THE JEWELS OF ELEGANCE

SNEHA JAIN

"

To all the Indians , not only by nationality but those at heart.
"

Contents

Contents

Foreword

I wrote my debut book during my last TEEN year, nineteen. It was launched in August 2020. The title of the book is "The Visionary Lights from a Dark Mind". It contains some easily readable poems on various topics. My second book was launched in July 2021. It is titled as "She-The Withered Flower".It is a collection of poems , which depict the various things that the female gender goes through. It is a step to raise voice against the cruelty , the girls and the women face in this world, hence showing how the female gender suffers yet blooms with a little sunshine of respect and love.

"The Jewels of Elegance " is my third book,wherein,I bring out the beauty of 28 states of India through poems.

I am thankful to my parents , my school and most importantly my college and the teachers for always supporting me and motivating me to do better in life.

Preface

ABOUT THE AUTHOR:-

Sneha Jain grew up in Karnal,Haryana, India. At present, she is 21 year old girl and an undergraduate in B.A English Honours . She is the author of 2 books . Her first book "The Visionary Lights from a Dark Mind" got reconised by a world record book. While her second book "She -The Withered Flower" got recognised by an Indian record book.

Her both the books are available on Amazon ,globally.

ABOUT THE BOOK:-

"The Jewels of Elegance" is a poetry book consisting of poems on 28 jewelsof India. The jewels that make India elegant.The states of India have the most important role in the existence of THE INCREDIBLE INDIA.

Acknowledgements

I would like to acknowledge the extraordinary debt I owe to my parents who have told me such wise things about life over the years.

I would not be able to achieve this day without the continual support of my school and the college faculties. The teachers of my college have been my constant motivation.

"The Visionary Lights From a Dark Mind"

"She-The Withered Flower"

1. The Kohinoor

The subtle,
Seventh largest state,
The Kohinoor of India.
The peaceful rivers howl,
all around,
The India's rice bowl.
Pearls of Hyderabad,
To Malkha's fabric,
Bargain and obtain ,
keeps up,
Though,
The enthusiasm unbridled.
The deific temples and
The magnificient forts,
A testament
To the rich antecedents.

2. The Emerald

The pristine picturesque,
and lush green,
The Northeast India's
Hidden gem.
The monastries,
symbolising
erudition and affluences.
The wildest,
least explored state,
The Land of
Dawn-Lit Mountains.
The snow capped peaks,
The feline species.
Towards the East,
The emeralds stream.

3. The Tourmaline

The stress relieving
organic tea,
exported worldwide.
The vibrant silk,
The oil drills,
The hills and the rivers,
The state's charmers.
A host to
The floristic wealth and
enormous faunal diversity,
A state,
spread with positivity.
The National parks,
The wildlife sancturies,
The tourists'
point of interest.

4. The Citrine

Ironically, the seat,
of the most prosperous heritage.
The vibrant cultural stage,
The Hindu pilgrimage core,
The state of power.
The silk fabrics,
The madhubani paintings,
overall,
The state of brightness.
The history of monks,
A powerful cleanser,
The strengthening endurance.

5. The Aquamarine

The widest waterfalls,
The exquisite landscapes,
Own every bit of serenity,
From the hill platues ,
To the Kapalik dance.
Adobe various tribes,
A state full of heritage sites.
Rich in minerals,
The state with,
well carved temples.

6. The Iolite

The crystal clear beaches,
The thrilling water sports,
The scrumptious sea food,
The lavish cruise,
The dazzling nightlife,
This state,
A tourist's paradise.
The holy churches,
The carnival festivals,
The christmas celebrations
A state with numerous
places of worships.

7. The Pure Gold

Birthplace
To the father of India,
The state ,
Opulent with godly places.
Over the beaches,
the temples sprinkled.
The land of traditions,
laced with heritage.
The flamboyant cuisine,
renowned for its taste.
The arrays of crafts,
The unusual tribal jewellery,
This state,
A Jewel of Western India.

8. The Lemon Quartz

The abode of God,
At the foothills
of Aravalli,
A small state set.
The heaven on earth,
standing tall ,
The achievements in agriculture,
Art and Culture.
Paddy and Wheat,
The farmers sweat.
The bread basket of the nation,
Agriculture,
The primary occupation.

9. The White Howlite

The land of braves,
The arid landscapes,
The land of Gods,
People rowing boats.
Fabrics in brillian hues,
The hilly morning views.
Residing in himalaya's lap,
The land of snow is the tag.

10. The Turquoise

The green ,
dense forest land,
Endowed with rich cultural heritage,
Bestowed with bounties of nature.
Kaleidoscope of past splendours,
A state of
captivating wildlife,
enthralling watefalls
and
A treasure -trove of mineral wealth.
Crowds of devotees,
The house of religious shrines.

11. The Aurum

The land of sandalwood,
One state many worlds.
India's electronic capitial,
The silicon valley Bangalore,
The garden city of India.
The state ,
A host to thirteen languages,
Known as the languages house.

12. The Ruby

The land of coconuts,
The tranquil backwaters,
The unspoiled beaches,
art forms and spices,
enhance the beauty of the state.
The high level of literacy,
and life expentancy,
The waving palms ,
The wide sandy shores,
The state a tropical paradise.

13. The Carnelian

The heart of India,
The magnificent tombs of Orccha,
The historic golden Gwalior,
The Khajuraho's sensual scruptures,
The ancient temples of ujjain,
Mandu,
The land of happiness.
The second largest,
Heartland state of nation.

14. The Jadeite

Aptly,
The gateway of India,
The land of lord Ganesha.
Ajanta, Ellora and Ellephanta,
The ancient cultural caves,
Flipping the historical page.
The Paithani sarees,
To Kolhapuri sandals,
All latest trends in fashion.
Palatial abode of bollywood stars,
The state offers ample fun
To the travelers.

15. The Marquise

The Switzerland of India,
The lush green meadows,
The aromactic tea estates,
The colourful communities,
living in harmony.
The folklore ,myths and legends,
A perfect tourist destination,

16. The Amethyst

The abode of clouds,
Speckled with big waterfalls,
And the abundant rainfall.
The limestone caves,
The perpetual clouds,
The state,
A bouquet of many identities,
The Scotland of East.

17. The Blue Spinel

The peninsula state,
The land of blue mountains.
The hills being crisscrossed,
by gushing rivers ,
high sparkling waterfalls.
The thick bamboo groves,
The narrow gorges,
The rugged terrains and rivers,
Enlighten a spark,
for outdoor activities.

18. The Kyanite

The falcon capital of the world,
The most obscure Indian state,
The land of festivals,
Shrouded in mystery,
Abounds in serene beauty.
The undulting state,
The land of dancing warriors.
The hypnotic beat of log drums,
The battle cry of Naga warriors,
mesmerise oneself.

19. The Hematite

The soul of India,
The land of temples,
The grandeur of architecture,
The glorious ancient history,
The temples depict.
The verdant forests,
The teeming wildlife,
A fascinating state.
The lakes and rivers,
wonder the nectar of Euphoria.

20. The Kunzite

The land of five rivers,
The place of Sikhism,
The mouth-watering dishes,
The culture is the richest.
Swathes of green fields,
Quaint contryside villages,
The most fertile state.
The colorful headwear,
The traditional footwear,
The state of hearts.

21. The Zircon

The land of kings,
Well-known for the ancient ruins.
The prosperous families,
Royalty painted with cultures,
For bravery and chivalry,
The state is known,
where numerous great warriors ,
were born.

22. The Ammolite

The second smallest state of India,
The dazzling waterfalls,
The virgin forests,
The alpine meadows,
The rhododendron flowers.
The state,
abounded in variety,
Flora and Fauna,
The endangered red panda,

23. The Eudialyte

The most urbanised state,
The blissful beaches,
The terrecotta figurines.
The splendid architecture,
The vast manufacturing sector.
This southern jewel,
The second largest state wealth.
Art,music and literature,
known for the civilised culture

24. The Lapis Lazuli

The youngest state,
A major part of Deccan plateau,
A pleasing climate,
India's seed capital,
The serene lakes,
The verdant woods,
A land of rich heritage,
The language,
renowned for the melody and grace.

25. The Dalmatian Jasper

The state of tribal culture,
The breathtaking scenic view,
A cultural reservoir.
The bountiful biodiversity,
The flushing meadows,
The irresistible charms.
A land locked state,
Bamboo forestry - a strength.

26. The Obsidian

The state of gods,
The composed Himalayas,
The spellbinding landscapes.
The snow -covered soaring peaks,
A plethora of places of adventure,
A home to,
The queen of hills,
The lake district of India.
All in all,
A place to purify the aura.

27. The Rose Quartz

The heartland of India,
Adobe to love stricken Agra,
Its capital,
The city of nawabs,
charm with authority.
A pilgrim centre,
Each religion looked after.
beautifies the India's diversity,
Well-known universally.

28. The Tiger's Eye

The fourth-most populous state,
Hosts the biggest mangroove forests.
Perpetually, the ongoing festival,
celebrating the human existence,
The abode of art and culture.
The state with broad networf of rivers,
Prominent for its sericulture,
A home to the man-eaters.

9 798887 045139

Printed by Libri Plureos GmbH in Hamburg, Germany